WE ARE OPEN
FROM 11AM-9PM
Tapas
Shakes
Daiquiris
Khmer Smiles

The Best of Friends
The Restaurant

Text by Gustav Auer, editing by Samantha Brown, design
by Ewan Clark, photography by Jim Mizerski & inspired by
all the students and teachers of Friends The Restaurant.

Printed in Cambodia by 3DGraphics Publishing

Published in December 2004
by Mith Samlanh/Friends,
Phnom Penh, Cambodia

Photographs © Jim Mizerski
Paintings © Mith Samlanh/Friends
Printed by 3D Graphics,
Phnom Penh, Cambodia

ISBN 0-9763607-0-5

Photo: Elfriede Wolfsberger © 2004

The Best of Friends
T h e   R e s t a u r a n t

215, Street 13
Phnom Penh, Cambodia
+855 12 802 072
www.streetfriends.org

Friends the Restaurant is non-profit and works as part of a programme for street children, their families and their community. All proceeds from the sale of this book will go directly back to Mith Samlanh/Friends.

 Contents

~ Meat dishes ~

~ Relishes & dressings ~

~ Desserts ~

~ Shakes & freezes, margaritas & daiquiris ~

bhpbilliton

BHP Billiton Petroleum is delighted to support the publication of *The Best of Friends The Restaurant*. Friends The Restaurant is a brilliantly conceived project that makes a real difference to the lives of many hundreds of street children in Phnom Penh. It is used to provide training and skills in the catering and hospitality industry. Visiting the restaurant was not only a gastronomic highlight of my wife Fran's and my visit to Cambodia, but it introduced us to this truly inspirational and very special place.

I recommend it to all visitors to Cambodia - it is not only a great place to go, but your visit will support the life saving and life changing work of Mith Samlanh/Friends. BHP Billiton Petroluem has supported Mith Samlanh/Friends for a number of years now.

This book includes a selection of the restaurant's most popular recipes. I am sure the publication of this recipe book will help to both publicise its good work and to raise funds.

I hope you enjoy making the delicious dishes in the book.

Philip Aiken
Group President Energy
BHP Billiton

Friends The Restaurant is one of the many projects of Mith Samlanh/Friends holistic service to street children. Some 10,000 to 20,000 children are living and working on the streets of Phnom Penh. Their numbers are rising because of poverty in the countryside and due to more and more parents falling sick and dying of AIDS-related diseases. Mith Samlanh/Friends supports these children as they reintegrate into society.

Mith Samlanh/Friends is a child-centered programme committed to the Convention on the Rights of the Child. We currently work with over 1,800 children per day within 12 different projects supported by over 200 Cambodian personnel. Our work falls into three categories.

The first covers reintegration projects, which involve:
- Working daily with the children directly on the streets of Phnom Penh;
- Running drop-in centres to provide short-term shelter and support to boys who work at night and to girls who just arrived in the city;
- Providing residential facilities to children who study at Mith Samlanh/Friends;
- Running a remedial primary school to provide innovative non-formal teaching at all levels of primary education;
- Running a training centre that provides a choice of 11 workshops organised as businesses such as restaurants and shops to allow students to have real-life experiences while training; and
- Supporting children who wish to return to their families and families to take responsibility for their children, as well as reintegrating children into public schools or helping them find employment.

The second category covers life skills education and supporting at-risk children, which involves:
- Providing children with comprehensive information about reproductive health, HIV/AIDS, drugs and human rights to allow them to protect themselves and make informed choices;
- Supporting children infected by HIV/AIDS – which comprises 15% of children in the training centre – with medical care and emotional support;
- Supporting children affected by AIDS – which is roughly 40% of the children arriving onto the streets – and organising their placement once they are orphaned;
- Promoting and implementing the Convention on the Rights of the Child and protecting children from physical and sexual abuse; and
- Providing children with information about the risk of drug use and strategies to reduce harm linked to drug use, along with alternatives to drug use, detoxification services and effective and sustainable rehabilitation choices.

The third category is capacity building of people working with street children. This involves:
- Training NGO, government and municipality professionals in working with and providing support to street children;
- Carrying out research and advocacy related to street children and issues such as drug use and working with street children; and
- Networking between organisations and agencies working with street children and on related issues such as drugs, child rights and the support of children affected by AIDS.

For more information please go to **www.streetfriends.org**   **MITH SAMLANH/FRIENDS**

Introduction

I was asked by Gustav Auer, the Chef (d'orchestre) behind Friends The Restaurant and this cookbook, to write this introduction. He asked me to talk about Friends and what has happened over the past 10 years...10 years! It is not easy to write about this since so much has happened: from the early days of the small organisation to the work carried out today with street children in Cambodia, Laos, Thailand, Myanmar and other countries in the world.

It was 1994 when three of us, Barbara Adams, Mark Turgesen and I, started Mith Samlanh, or "Friends" in English. I arrived with Barbara from Paris on my way to Japan and we decided to stay in Cambodia for a few weeks. It is difficult to describe Cambodia at that time: the rare electricity, the regular gunshots, the roads with holes so deep one could drown in them during the rainy season. War was in the jungle and mines were everywhere – they actually de-mined the corner of my street one month after my arrival. Most of all there was extreme poverty for everyone and overwhelming wealth and power for a few.

One night coming out late from a restaurant at the Central Market run by an eccentric Singaporean, I stumbled over a row of more than 20 children sleeping on cardboard on the footpath. I remember seeing a big black expensive car drive by, and this really upset me. I had seen street children before in Asia, but this time it really hit me: how could it be possible that in a country with so many organisations and so much donor money, children, the future of Cambodia, could be ignored like that? Wasn't this unjust and actually undermining all the efforts of development of Cambodia?

We started bringing food to the children: bread with ham, bananas and clean water. This is when we met Mark who, like us, was upset. He was cooking rice in his hotel room and distributing it to the children. We met and sat down faced with an important issue: with the three of us and various others providing food, the children received up to eight meals a day... Of course they were happy to stay on the streets! What we were doing was actually harmful. We then had to make a decision. Either we just stopped, ignored it all and I left for Japan, or we had to do something constructive. After some discussions, and because we were young, full of hope and certainly a little crazy, we decided to go for the constructive approach. I remember not being able to sleep for three nights as I realised the decision would influence the next few years of my life – little did I know how much change it would actually bring.

Because Mark and Barbara had jobs, they asked me to be in charge of running the organisation. With the help of some Cambodian friends, we met with the children in the evenings and started talking and identifying what they wanted and needed. I used my savings and contributions from Mark and Barbara to rent and furnish a small house by the Russian Market with a large common room, two dormitories, showers, a kitchen and a small classroom.

On August 1, 1994, with a team of three Cambodians, some of whom still work with Mith Samlanh now, we opened the centre. I remember being outside the house seeing the first 17 children arrive on cyclos. This first night was chaotic: suddenly our vision came to life. There was laughter and fun. There was music and dancing. I was happy but stressed. Eventually I went home, hoping that the first night with the Cambodian team would go smoothly. I spent my days and evenings at the centre, played soccer in the living room, encouraged the children to join the classroom, went on outings and stressed over money.

After 10 days, all the children had left except for one.

This is when the team and I learnt our first and most important lesson: our mistake was that we thought we knew what was best for the children and wanted to provide what we thought they needed. We had bought mattresses; they wanted to sleep on the tiles, because they were cooler. We had prepared a classroom; the young people did not care about literacy, they wanted a job. We learnt to listen to the children and from then on, they have been guiding our work. We adapted to them, instead of expecting them to adapt to us. We changed the system, developed our work on the streets and accepted children for the day time only, encouraging them to return home. Their numbers started growing – fast.

For two years we struggled. I worked at night, took part-time jobs and received small private donations to fund the operation. One Friday night I was too depressed and decided that it was time to call it quits. No money was coming in and the team and I were exhausted from overwork. The next Monday, I received a phone call from Save the Children Australia announcing the impossible: Ausaid, the Australian government's aid agency, offered to fund Friends for three years.

The rest is history.

We were able to build Mith Samlanh's 12 projects, among them the much-needed training centre. Cooking was one of the first skills among 11 others that we taught. Gustav came to teach as a volunteer on a regular basis. Unfortunately, because of lack of money he decided to return to Canada in 1999. A few days afterwards, I accessed money from the European Commission and DOH-International to start a business. I sent Gustav a loaded email asking him if he knew of anyone who would be interested in becoming the trainer for this project. He jumped on the next plane back.

With the children we designed what became Friends The Restaurant, featuring its trademark colourful walls, the children's paintings hanging on them and the tapas menu of East meets West flavours. We focused on simple yet tasty dishes that were easy to teach the children and yummy to eat. It opened in February 2001.

Over the years Friends The Restaurant has become very successful. More clients have visited and we have trained more young people. Many of them now work in restaurants around Phnom Penh and other cities of Cambodia. We are very proud of them.

Many of our customers have asked for a recipe book. We wanted to make something beautiful and waited until 2004 when Gustav got a great team together: Ewan for the fun design, Jim for the gorgeous photos and Sam for working with Gustav on editing the recipes.

We hope that you will enjoy the book as much as we enjoyed making it. Try the recipes and enjoy the result. But remember, Gustav and the students continue to create new meals and new shakes: you need to come and taste them and give us your opinion so we can prepare our second book!

Thank you, Dana, for supporting me over the years.

Thank you to all of you who made this adventure possible. There is still more to do.

Sébastien Marot
Phnom Penh, October 2004

Khmer beef lok lak and **vegetable fried rice.** See page 86.

Cambodians love to share their meals. Food is served up on large plates and everybody helps themselves - it's so much more fun this way. And they only eat with their spoons. Forks are used for serving.

Khmer-style fried fish with **lemongrass.**
See page 66.

Vegetarian **Dishes**

Sun-dried Tomato Hummus on Crispy Wonton Wrappers

Serves 6-8

480g can chickpeas, drained and rinsed
4 tbsp extra virgin olive oil
1 tsp tahini
3 tsp sun-dried tomatoes, finely chopped

2 tsp fresh basil, chopped
1 tsp fresh lemon juice
1 garlic clove, finely chopped
½ tsp ground cumin
salt and pepper to taste
crispy wonton wrappers

Place chickpeas, olive oil and tahini in food processor and blend well.

Place mixture into bowl, mix in remaining ingredients and serve on top of crispy wonton wrappers or as a dip.

Try with: An ice-cold beer.

Friends' Famous Smoky Eggplant Dip

4 Japanese eggplants
4 tbsp extra virgin olive oil
3 tbsp good-quality mayonnaise, homemade is best
1 tbsp fresh lemon juice
4 garlic cloves, finely chopped
2 tbsp fresh coriander, chopped
salt and pepper to taste
1 tbsp tomatoes, peeled, seeded and diced
1 tbsp spring onions, sliced

Grill the eggplant until blackened. Once cool, peel off the burned skin and dice. Blend the eggplant, olive oil and mayonnaise until smooth and creamy. Place into bowl, then add the lemon juice, garlic, coriander, salt and pepper. Top with the tomatoes and sliced spring onions.

Makes 8-10 servings.

Try with: Assorted raw vegetables or toasted French bread with a glass of Chardonnay. Makes the perfect BBQ or picnic dip.

Curried Pumpkin Soup with Coriander

Serves 4-6

For the curry paste:
2 lemongrass stems, sliced
1 tsp fresh turmeric, peeled
1 tsp fresh galangal, peeled
zest ½ kaffir lime
4 Asian shallots
4 garlic cloves
3 small chillies, seeded
1 tbsp Indian curry powder
**1 tbsp Vietnamese curry
powder (*ca ro bo*)**

120g unsalted butter
2 medium onions, diced
2 celery stalks, diced
1½ litres chicken or vegetable stock
**1 small pumpkin (about 1kg),
peeled, seeded and cubed**
**1 cup coconut milk or coconut
cream**
1 tbsp palm or brown sugar
salt and pepper to taste
1 small bunch coriander, chopped

To make the curry paste, place all the ingredients into a mortar and pound until a paste. Set aside.

In a large saucepan, melt the butter, add the onions and celery and sauté for a few minutes on medium-high heat. Add the curry paste and fry until very fragrant, which should take about 2 minutes. Do not overcook.

Add the stock and pumpkin. Cover and simmer for 45 minutes. Reserving a few teaspoons for the garnish, add the coconut cream and sugar, salt and pepper, and simmer for 10 more minutes.

Blend the soup in a food processor and serve drizzled with remaining coconut cream and top with coriander.

Try with: Garlic croutons sprinkled on top. This is how we serve it in the restaurant.

Grilled Vegetable and Pasta Salad with Goat Cheese

4 ripe tomatoes, sliced
1 Japanese eggplant, sliced
1 medium zucchini, sliced
1 red pepper, sliced
virgin olive oil
400g rottini pasta
½ cup fresh basil
200g goat cheese

For the dressing:
½ cup extra virgin olive oil
4 tbsp red wine vinegar
4 garlic cloves, finely chopped
salt and pepper to taste

Serves 4

Brush the vegetables with a little virgin olive oil and grill. Put aside to cool. Cook the pasta in a large saucepan of boiling, salted water until *al dente*, drain and set aside to cool.

Place the dressing ingredients into a glass jar with a lid and shake.

Combine all the ingredients except the goat cheese in a bowl. Divide between 4 plates and sprinkle with chunks of the cheese. Garnish with basil leaves.

Try with: A crisp rosé wine.

Stir-fried Tomato Wedges with Mint

4 tbsp olive oil

6 large, ripe tomatoes, cut into wedges

1 cup fresh mint

1 tbsp fresh lime juice

salt and pepper to taste

Heat olive oil in a frying pan over high heat, add tomatoes and mint and stir-fry for 1-2 minutes. Add the lime juice, salt and pepper.

Try with: Grilled fish or alone as a refreshing summer salad.

Serves 4

Sautéed Leek and Apple

¼ cup unsalted butter

3 medium leeks, sliced

3 Granny Smith apples, peeled and cut into thin wedges

salt and pepper to taste

Melt the butter in frying pan. Add leeks and sauté for a few minutes. Add apples and fry for 1 more minute. Season with salt and pepper.

Try with: Grilled pork chops.

Serves 4

Carrots with Coriander

6 medium carrots, peeled and cut into thick julienned slices

¼ cup unsalted butter

1 bunch fresh coriander, chopped

salt and pepper to taste

Blanch carrots in boiling water for 1-2 minutes, drain, place on ice to keep the colour and set aside. Melt the butter in frying pan. Add carrots and sauté for 1 minute. Add coriander, salt and pepper.

Try with: Roast turkey.

Serves 4

Asian-style Mango Coleslaw with Sesame and Lime

Serves 4

2 mangoes, not too ripe, peeled and shredded
½ medium-sized Chinese cabbage, shredded
1 red pepper, thinly sliced
1 medium cucumber, peeled, seeded and thinly sliced
½ red onion, thinly sliced
2 tbsp fresh Thai basil, chopped
1 tbsp black sesame seeds
1 tbsp white sesame seeds

For the dressing:

250g Thai sweet chilli sauce
1 tbsp fish sauce
1 tbsp sesame oil
1 tbsp lime juice

Place the dressing ingredients into a glass jar with a lid and shake well. In a bowl, combine all the coleslaw ingredients except the sesame seeds and toss through the dressing.
Divide between 4 plates and sprinkle with the seeds.

Try with: Grilled fish or chicken, or as a light lunch on its own.

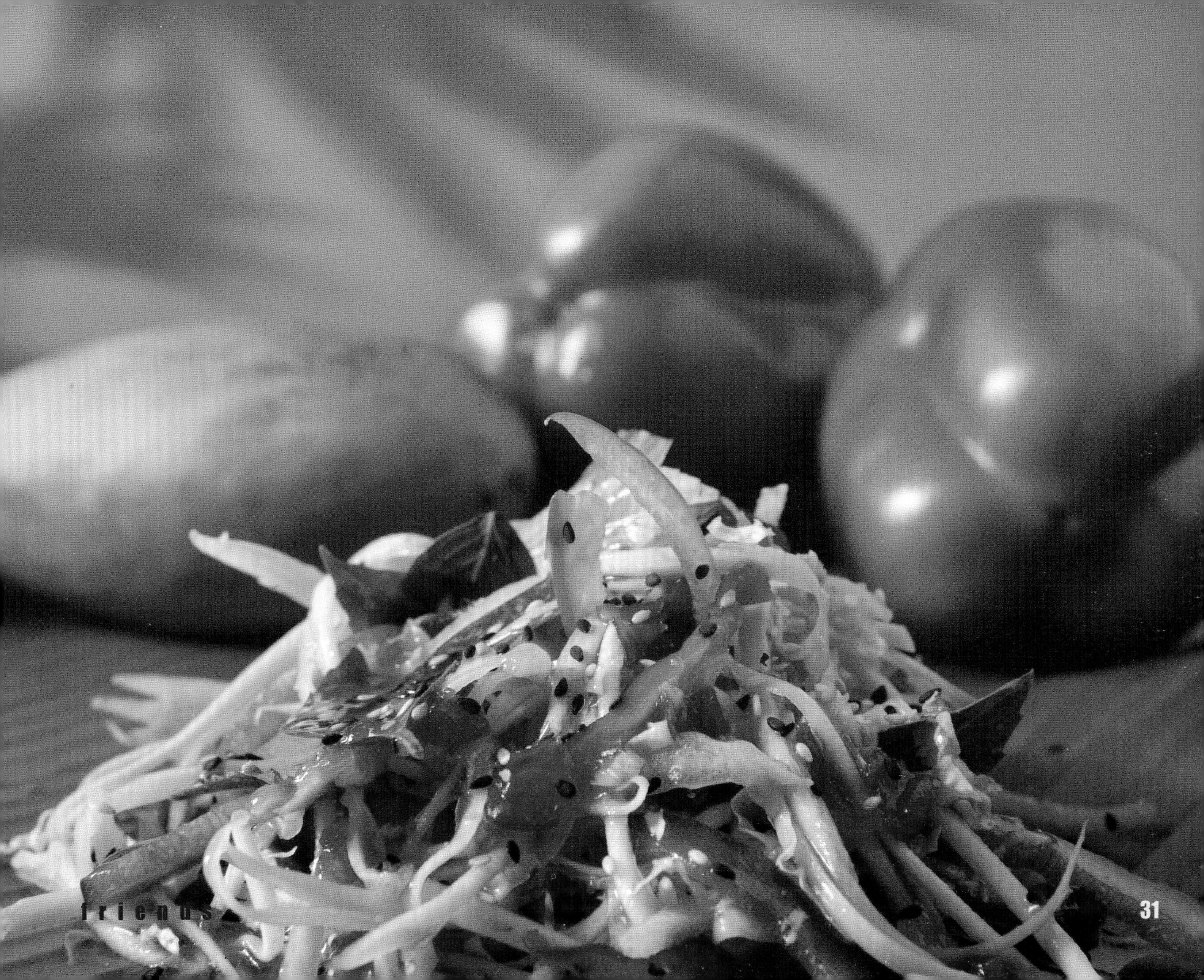

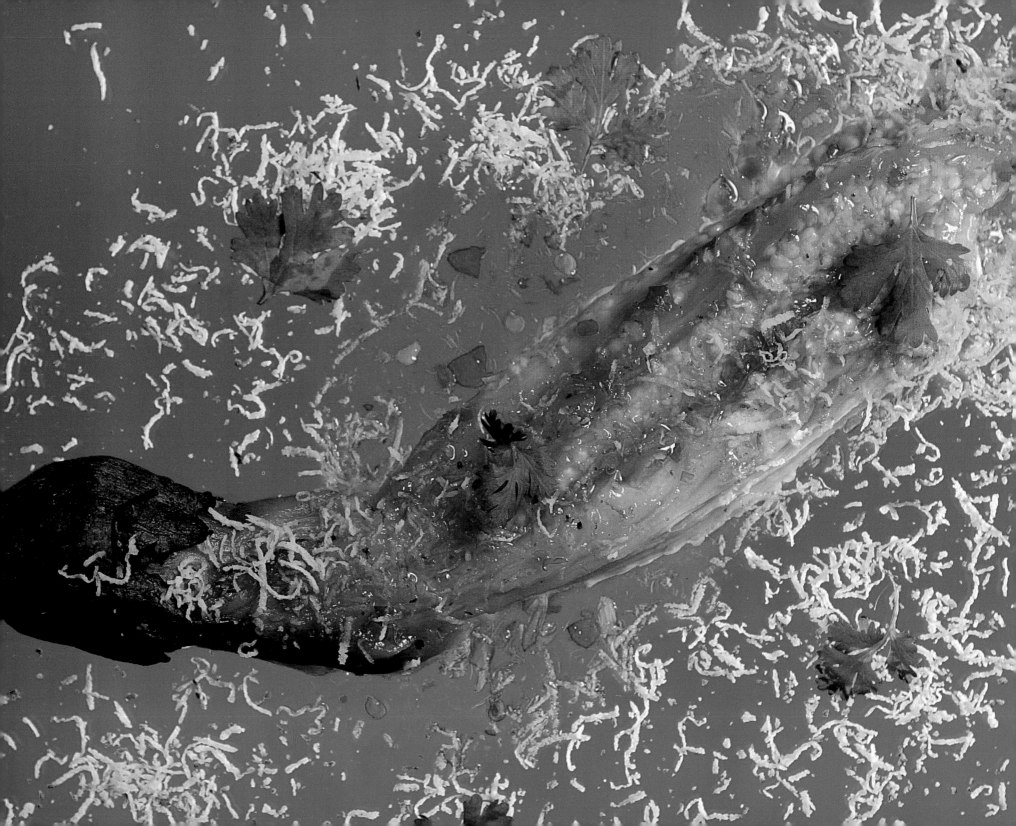

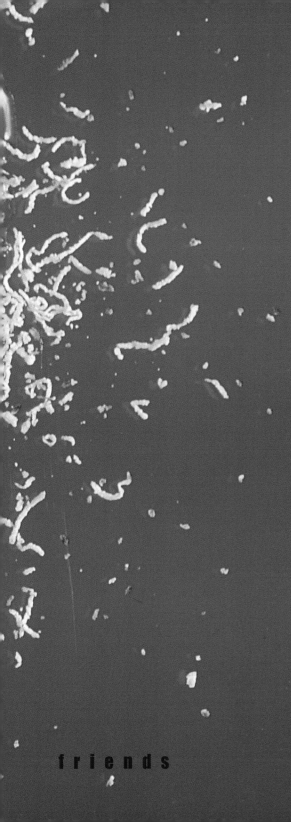

Grilled Eggplant Salad
with **Toasted Coconut**

Prick eggplants for they EXPLODE

Serves 4

4 tbsp shredded coconut
6 Japanese eggplants
4 tbsp fresh coriander, chopped

For the dressing:
4 tbsp fish sauce
4 tbsp sugar
2 tbsp fresh lime juice
1 tbsp rice vinegar
4 garlic cloves, finely chopped
2 red chillies

Dry-fry the coconut in a heavy-based frying pan until golden and set aside to cool.

Grill the eggplant until blackened. Once cool, peel off the burned skin and dice.

Combine all the dressing ingredients into a bowl.

Divide the eggplant between 4 plates, spoon over dressing and top with toasted coconut and coriander.

Khmers eat this as a side dish or topped with stir-fried minced pork as a main course, with rice on the side. Otherwise, this is perfect with toasted French bread.

Mushroom and Leek Spring

2 tbsp extra virgin olive oil
1 large onion, finely chopped
6 Asian shallots
4 medium leeks, finely chopped
300g fresh mushrooms, finely chopped
(if possible, use wild mushrooms as the
taste is fantastic)
salt and pepper to taste
juice of ½ lemon
2 tbsp Worcestershire sauce
1 bunch fresh mixed herbs, such as mint,
coriander, marjoram and basil, chopped
16-20 pieces rice paper
oil for deep frying

For the mayonnaise:
4 tbsp mayonnaise
1 tsp lemon juice
1 small bunch coriander, roughly chopped

Rolls with Lemon Mayonnaise

Heat olive oil in large frying pan, add onion and shallots and sauté until transparent. Add leeks and fry for 5 minutes on a medium-high heat. Add mushrooms and fry until there is hardly any liquid left, which should take 15-20 minutes. Stir in salt and pepper, lemon juice, Worcestershire sauce and herbs. Set aside to cool.

Brush rice paper with water, spoon mushroom mixture on and roll. Deep fry on medium-high heat until golden. Drain on paper towels before serving as soon as possible, with the mayonnaise mixture on the side.

very good without deep frying

Try with: A crisp white wine.

Makes 16-20.

"My favourite food to cook is spring rolls. I like them with mushroom and leeks, but they're also good with a mix of carrot and taro."

Kim Sophorn, 18, hot kitchen

Sweet Potato Fries with Curry Mayonnaise

~ vegetable oil for deep-frying ~ 4 medium sweet potatoes, peeled and cut into fries ~
1 cup mayonnaise ~ 1 tbsp Indian curry powder ~
juice of ¼ lemon ~ ½ small bunch fresh coriander, chopped ~

Heat the oil and deep-fry sweet potatoes on medium heat for about 3 minutes. Drain on paper towels. Mix the mayonnaise, curry powder, lemon juice and coriander together and serve in a bowl on the side.

Serves 4

Try with: An ice-cold beer.

friends

friends

39

Khmer Fish Soup
with Tamarind

2 cups coconut milk
1 tbsp shrimp paste
1½ tbsp fish sauce
600g firm white fish fillets, such as sea bass, cut into cubes
½ cup tamarind juice (to make, soak 100g tamarind pulp in ½ cup hot water)
2 cups fish or vegetable stock
½ cup roasted and crushed peanuts, unsalted
1 tsp palm or brown sugar
salt to taste

For the lemongrass paste:

3 lemongrass stems, sliced
4 garlic cloves
1 small piece fresh galangal, peeled
1 small piece fresh turmeric, peeled
4 kaffir lime leaves
small piece kaffir lime peel

Pound these ingredients to a paste in a mortar and set aside.

Boil half the coconut milk in a large saucepan until it turns creamy. Add the lemongrass paste and fry for 1-2 minutes. Add the shrimp paste, fish sauce and fish and fry on medium heat for 2 minutes.

Add the remainder of the coconut milk, tamarind juice and stock, and simmer for 5 more minutes. Stir in peanuts, sugar and salt. Do not boil the soup again.

Try with: Steamed white rice.

Instead of shrimp paste, Cambodians use *prahok*, a fermented fish paste that is a staple in Khmer cuisine. Its very strong flavour makes it difficult for many foreigners to appreciate.

Serves 4

Crispy Prawn Wontons with Sweet Chilli Sauce

200g prawns, cleaned, peeled and chopped

1 small bunch fresh coriander, finely chopped

1 tbsp oyster sauce

2 garlic cloves, finely chopped

½ tsp sugar

salt and pepper to taste

16 wonton wrappers

vegetable oil for deep frying

½ cup Thai sweet chilli sauce

Combine prawns, coriander, oyster sauce, garlic, sugar, salt and pepper together and refrigerate for about an hour. Spoon teaspoonfuls of the mixture into the centre of each wonton wrapper. Brush the edges of the wontons with a little water and form into parcels. Deep fry on medium-high heat until golden, which should take about 2 minutes. Drain on paper towels and serve immediately, with chilli sauce for dipping on the side. **Makes 16**. These are great for a cocktail party.

Try with: Your favourite cocktail.

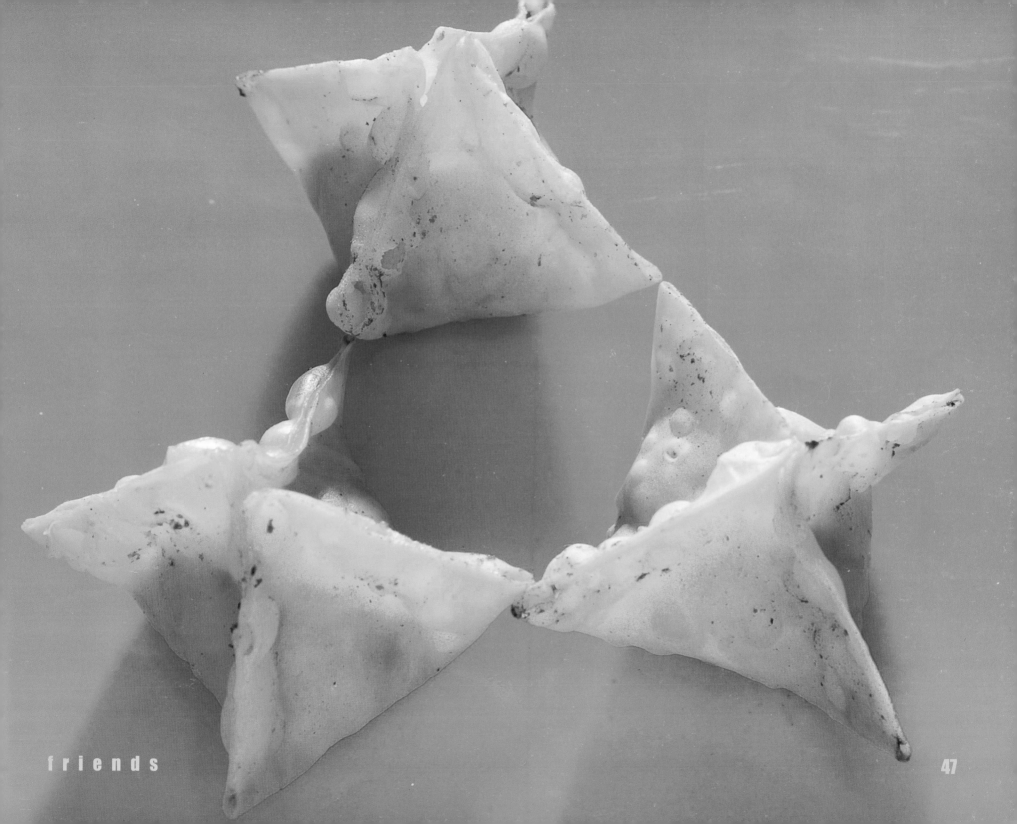

friends

Fish and Potato Cakes with Roasted Red Pepper Sauce

Makes about 12 small cakes or enough for 4 servings

~ 2 medium leeks, thinly sliced ~ few tspns olive oil ~ 250g fish
fillet, boiled and broken into small chunks ~ 3 medium potatoes,
boiled, peeled and grated ~ 1 Tabasco splash ~ 2 spring onions,
sliced ~ salt and pepper to taste ~ ½ cup of olive oil, for
frying ~ lemon wedges ~

For the sauce:
~ 2 large red peppers ~ 2 tbsp red wine vinegar ~ 2 tbsp sugar ~
¼ cup extra virgin olive oil ~ salt and pepper to taste ~

To make the sauce, roast the whole peppers in an oven on very high heat for about 30 minutes. Turn the peppers frequently and allow the skin to burn black. Remove from oven and place in a bowl. Cover with plastic wrap while the peppers cool to ease peeling. Peel and seed the peppers. Blend with remaining sauce ingredients in a food processor until creamy. This can be made up to one day ahead and stored in the fridge.

Fry the leeks in a few teaspoons of olive oil and set aside to cool. Place all the ingredients, including the leeks, into a bowl, gently mixing together. Shape them into small cakes and fry in olive oil on medium heat on each side for 2-3 minutes. Drain well on paper towels. Serve on top of the chilled or room-temperature red pepper sauce and garnish with a lemon wedge.

Try with: A good Australian Chardonnay.

Grilled Fish with Salsa Verde

Grilled Fish with Salsa Verde

1 cup fresh herbs, such as basil, mint, marjoram and thyme, chopped
2 tbsp capers, chopped
1 garlic clove, finely chopped
4 tbsp extra virgin olive oil
2 tbsp sherry vinegar
salt and pepper to taste
4 x 150g fish fillets
juice of ½ lemon
olive oil
1 tomato, peeled, seeded and diced
1 tbsp spring onions, thinly sliced

Serves 4

To make the salsa verde, mix the herbs, capers, garlic, olive oil and vinegar together in a bowl. Season with salt and pepper and chill.

Baste the fish with lemon juice, salt, pepper and olive oil. Grill.

Place a fish fillet on each of 4 plates, top with the chilled salsa verde and garnish with diced tomatoes and spring onions.

Try with: A crisp white wine.

friends

53

Marinated Fish Salad with Lime and Coriander

Serves 4

400g firm white fish fillets, thinly sliced
½ cup fresh lime juice
½ cup each of Thai basil, mint and coriander
1 large green pepper, thinly sliced
½ English cucumber, thinly sliced
2 tbsp roasted and crushed peanuts, unsalted

For the dressing:
1 cup marinade (see method)
3 tbsp fresh galangal, chopped
3 tbsp hot water
1 tbsp palm or brown sugar
2 tbsp fish sauce
1 garlic clove, chopped
salt to taste

Marinate the fish fillets in lime juice for 20 minutes. Drain and use marinade for dressing.

For the dressing, place the galangal into a mortar and pound into a paste. Add water, mix and drain through a sieve, reserving juice. Combine the marinade, galangal juice, palm sugar and fish sauce and bring to boil. Simmer strongly for 5 minutes and set aside to cool. Add garlic and salt.

Mix remaining salad ingredients together, except peanuts, and toss through dressing. Sprinkle with peanuts and serve.

Try with: A chilled Riesling.

Khmer Seafood Soup with Lime

Serves 4

~ 4 cups chicken or seafood stock ~ 2 cups coconut juice (not milk) ~ 2 lemongrass stems, cut into chunks ~ 100g fresh prawns, peeled and cleaned ~ 100g scallops ~ 100g sea bass or any other firm white fish fillet, cubed ~ 100g mussels or clams, cleaned well ~ 1 tbsp fish sauce ~ 4 tbsp tamarind juice (to make, soak 25g tamarind pulp in 4 tbsp hot water) ~ ½ tsp sugar ~ juice of 1 lime ~ 1 cup fresh mixed herbs, such as Thai basil, coriander and mint, chopped ~ 1 small red chilli, chopped ~

"This seafood soup is fast and easy and gives you plenty of energy. Guys should drink it with a beer, and women could try a coconut and pineapple shake."

Oom Socheat, 20, hot kitchen

Bring stock to the boil, add coconut juice and lemongrass and simmer for 10-15 minutes on medium-low heat. Add the prawns, scallops, fish and mussels and simmer for 3-4 minutes.

Take off the heat and stir in fish sauce, tamarind juice, sugar, lime and most of the herbs. Do not heat up again as it will lose taste and colour. Divide into soup bowls or empty coconut shells and garnish with chilli and the remainder of the herbs.

This is a big hit in the restaurant.

Stir-fried **Clams** with Tamarind and **Spicy Basil**

Serves 4

4 tbsp olive oil
8 garlic cloves, chopped
4 tbsp oyster sauce
2 kg fresh clams, cleaned well
½ cup Chinese wine
½ cup chicken or clam stock

3 small chillies, seeded and sliced thinly
2 tbsp palm or brown sugar
¼ cup tamarind juice (to make, soak 50g tamarind pulp in ¼ cup hot water)
1 bunch spicy or Thai basil

Heat olive oil in wok and add garlic. Fry for a few seconds and add oyster sauce and clams. Fry for 1 minute. Add Chinese wine, stock, chillies, sugar and tamarind juice. Fry for 2 more minutes or until clams open. Mix in the basil quickly and serve immediately.

Try with: Crusty French bread to dip into the sauce.

Khmers like to eat this dish as a snack with beer.

friends

Lemon and Garlic Squid

Serves 4

4 tbsp olive oil
8 garlic cloves, finely
chopped
600g squid, cleaned and
sliced
juice of 1 lemon
2 tbsp Worcestershire sauce
2 tbsp spring onions, sliced
2 tbsp tomatoes, seeded and
diced
salt and pepper to taste

Heat olive oil in frying pan and add garlic, frying until lightly browned. Add squid and fry for 1 minute on high heat. Do not overcook. Add lemon juice, Worcestershire sauce, spring onions, tomatoes, salt and pepper and sauté.

This dish makes great tapas, served with wine. Serve on slices of toasted French bread or toss with some pasta to have as a full meal.

Mixed Greens with Prawns in Cumin and Coriander Dressing

~ assorted greens, such as rocket, endives and butter lettuce ~
400g prawns, peeled and cooked ~ 4 Asian shallots, thinly sliced ~

For the dressing:
~ 2 tbsp mild Spanish paprika powder ~ ½ cup extra virgin olive oil ~ 2 tbsp lemon juice ~ 2 tbsp red wine vinegar ~ 2 tbsp sugar syrup ~ ¼ cup prawn stock, left over from boiling the prawns, cooled ~ 1 tbsp ground cumin, toasted ~ salt and pepper to taste ~ 2 tbsp fresh coriander, chopped ~
2 tbsp fresh parsley, chopped ~

To make the dressing, blend all ingredients except the coriander and parsley in a food processor. Add the herbs and chill. Dressing can be kept in the fridge for up to 4 days. Shake well before use.

Divide the greens between 4 plates and top with the prawns and shallots. Drizzle with the dressing.

Try with: A fruit shake.

This is a big lunchtime seller in the restaurant.   **Serves 4**

friends

Khmer-style Fried Fish
with **Lemongrass**

See page 17

Serves 4

1 lemongrass stem
1 whole fish, such as red snapper or rainbow trout, 1-2 kg, cleaned and gutted
2 cups vegetable oil, for frying

To serve:
2 cucumbers, sliced
lettuce leaves
bean sprouts
1 small bunch fresh Thai basil
1 small bunch fresh mint

For the dipping sauce:
Use 1 portion of the pomelo salad dressing on page 72 with 4 tbsp crushed peanuts added

Squeeze the lemongrass stem in half and stuff into the mouth of the fish. Do not add any salt or the fish will dry out. Heat vegetable oil in a large wok and fry the whole fish for about 5-7 minutes on each side.

Arrange the vegetables and herbs on a large plate and place the fish next to them, with the dipping sauce on the side in a separate bowl. To eat, take a lettuce leaf, add a slice of cucumber, some mint, bean sprouts, Thai basil and a piece of fish. Roll it up, dip in the sauce and munch.

The only way to eat this is with your hands, sharing it with others, while sitting on a bamboo mat with some steamed rice on the side. Khmer style!

friends

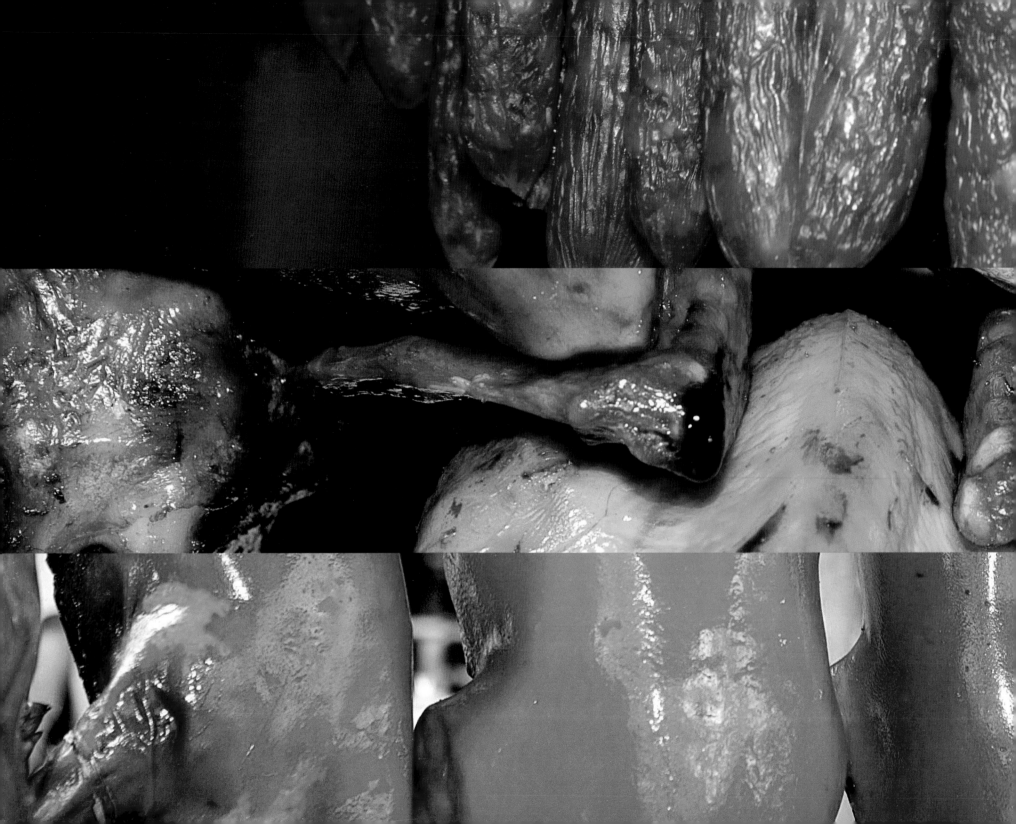

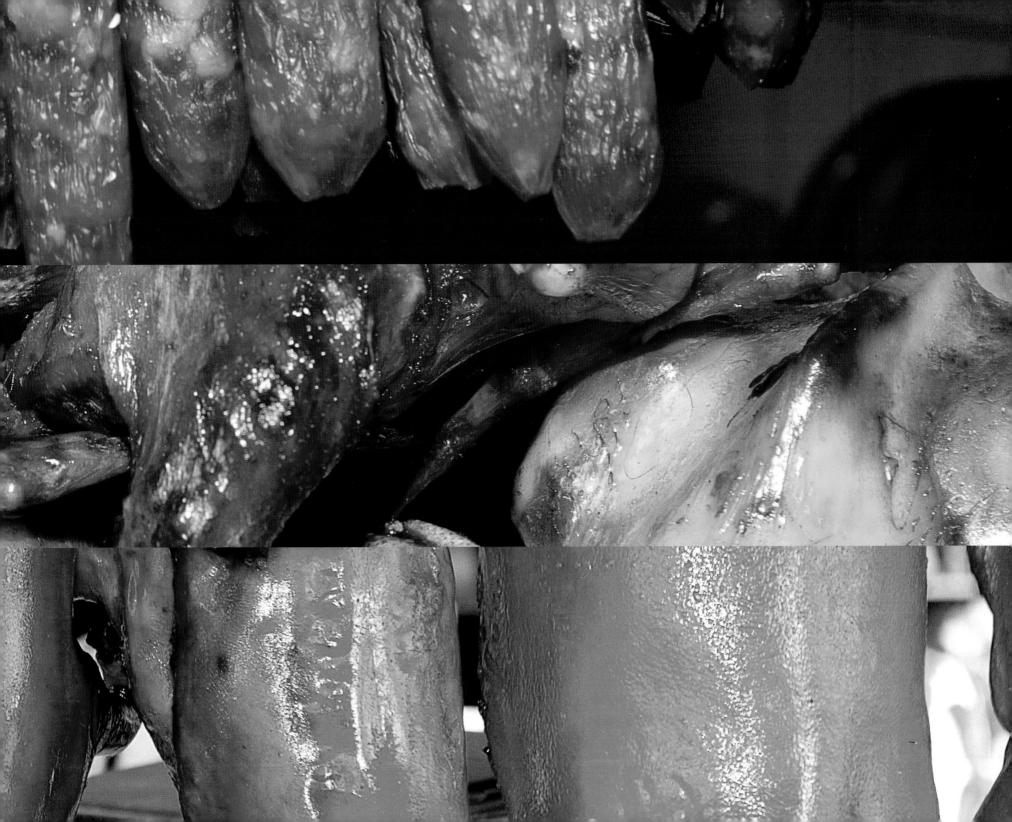

Friends' Famous Khmer Chicken Curry

Serves 4

1 tsp fresh galangal, peeled
1 tsp fresh turmeric, peeled
4 lemongrass stems, sliced
6 medium Asian shallots, peeled
zest of ½ kaffir lime
½ tsp star anise powder
4 garlic cloves, finely chopped
1 tbsp dried chillies, seeded
and soaked in water for 5 minutes
1 litre coconut milk
2 tbsp fish sauce
½ tsp shrimp paste
400g chicken,
from breast or leg, cubed
2 medium potatoes, peeled
and cut into 8 pieces each
chicken stock, if needed
1 tbsp palm sugar
1 tbsp Vietnamese
curry powder (*ca ro bo*)
1 medium onion, sliced
100g Chinese or French green
beans
salt to taste

Place the galangal, turmeric, lemongrass, shallots, zest, star anise powder and garlic into a mortar and pound into a paste. Chop the soaked chillies into a paste.

Bring half the coconut milk to the boil and reduce until most of the liquid is gone. Add the paste and fry until fragrant. Add the chilli paste, fish sauce and shrimp paste. Mix well and add the chicken. Stir well again. Add the potatoes and remainder of the coconut milk and boil for 5 minutes. If needed, add some chicken stock to make sure the curry is covered with enough liquid. Add palm sugar, curry powder, onion , beans and salt, then simmer for 15 more minutes.

Try with: Steamed rice or crusty French bread.

"My recommendation is Friends' famous Khmer chicken curry. It's real Cambodian food!"

Sok Heng, 23, waiter

friends

71

Pomelo Salad with Grilled Chicken and Fresh Mint

Serves 4

2 medium pomelo, peeled and broken into small pieces, or substitute with grapefruit
4 boneless chicken breasts, grilled and thinly sliced
small bunch fresh mint, chopped

For the dressing:
4 tbsp fish sauce
4 tbsp sugar
2 tbsp fresh lime juice
1 tbsp rice vinegar
4 garlic cloves, finely chopped
2 red chillies, chopped
1/3 cup hot water

To make the dressing, mix all the ingredients and chill. The mixture will keep in the fridge for up to 3 days.

Divide the pomelo between 4 plates. Add the chicken, top with mint and drizzle with the dressing.

Try with: A chilled white wine.

Tip: The dressing also works well as a dipping sauce for the spring rolls on page 34.

friends

Khmer Pork and Papaya Salad Sandwich

Serves 4

½ large green papaya, shredded
1 medium carrot, shredded
6 Asian shallots, thinly sliced
3 chillies, seeded and thinly sliced
600g pork fillet, sliced into medallions
salt and pepper to taste
4 sticks French bread
4 tsp Dijon mustard
4 tbsp mayonnaise

For the dressing:
Use the pomelo salad dressing recipe on page 72.

Mix the papaya, carrots, shallots and chillies with the dressing and set aside.

Season the pork with salt and pepper and grill on a barbecue until well done. Toast the bread on both sides on the barbecue. Slice lengthways in half. Spread with mustard and mayonnaise, fill with the papaya salad and pork. Serve immediately.

Try with: A Cambodian Angkor beer.

Serves 1

150g beef tenderloin, best cut
salt and pepper to taste
1 tsp oyster sauce
2 thick slices of onion
4 thick slices of tomato
1 tsp Dijon mustard
1 tsp mayonnaise
few lettuce leaves
bread roll, French or any other style

Brush the beef with salt, pepper and oyster sauce and grill until done to your liking, but make sure you don't overcook it. Sprinkle salt and pepper on the onion and tomato and add to grill.

Slice the roll in half and spread mustard and mayonnaise on both halves. Assemble the lettuce, tomato, onion and beef on the bread and serve immediately.

Try with: An ice cold beer.

FRIENDS' GRILLED STEAK SANDWICH

Chicken, Mango and Cashew Stir-Fry

Serves 4

~ 2 tbsp vegetable oil ~ 2 garlic cloves, chopped ~ 600g skinless, boneless chicken breast, sliced ~ 2 tbsp Chinese wine or dry sherry ~ 2 tbsp oyster sauce ~ 1 tsp corn flour ~ 1½ cups chicken stock ~ 1 tsp sugar ~ 2 mangoes, not too ripe, peeled and sliced into 1cm-thick pieces ~ ½ cup roasted cashew nuts, unsalted ~ salt and pepper to taste ~ spring onions, sliced ~

Heat vegetable oil in wok. Add garlic, fry until fragrance is released and add chicken. Fry for 2 minutes and add wine and oyster sauce. Sauté. Add corn flour to the chicken stock and then add to chicken mixture, frying 1 more minute. Add sugar, mangoes, cashew nuts, salt and pepper, mix and serve immediately, garnished with the spring onions.

Try with: Steamed rice.

"It's very hard to make a mistake with this stir-fry. Mangoes are my favourite fruit and are good in this dish but make sure you don't cook them for too long. "

Sothkim Yuri, 18, hot kitchen

1 onion, diced
4 tbsp olive oil
300g ground pork
300g ground beef
100g breadcrumbs
1 tbsp tomato paste
1 egg
4 garlic cloves, chopped
1 tbsp Dijon mustard
2 tbsp Worcestershire sauce
salt and pepper to taste
spring onions, sliced

For the sauce:
½ cup honey
6 garlic cloves, chopped
1 tbsp soy sauce
1 cup BBQ sauce
2 tbsp tomato sauce

Fry the onions in 2 tbsp of the olive oil until translucent. Set aside to cool.

Mix together the remainder of the meatball ingredients, including the onions, very well.

Form the mixture into small balls, wetting your hands to make it easier.

Heat remainder of olive oil in a frying pan. Add meatballs and shallow-fry on medium heat for about 2-3 minutes on each side. Drain on paper towels.

To make the sauce, combine all ingredients and heat in frying pan. Add the meatballs back and simmer for 1-2 minutes more. Serve garnished with spring onions.

We have had this dish on our standard menu since opening in February 2001. It is our best-selling menu item. Kids LOVE them!

Honey Garlic
Meatballs

friends

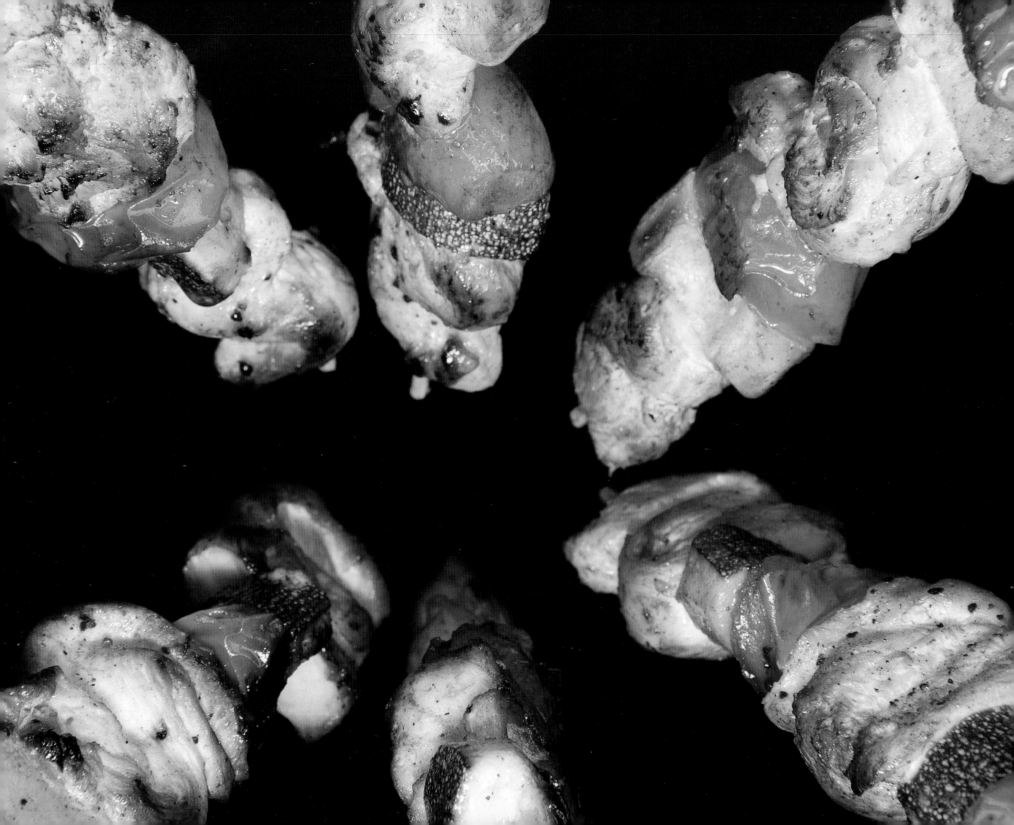

Asian-style Chicken and **Veggie Kebabs**

Serves 4

Thread chicken, zucchini and whole tomatoes onto skewers and set aside. If using wooden skewers, soak them in water for half an hour beforehand to ensure they don't burn.

Mix the marinade ingredients together and pour over the kebabs. Marinate for at least 2 hours in the fridge before grilling.

Try with: Pineapple salsa. In the restaurant, we serve them with papaya and mint relish, on page 89.

600g boneless chicken breast, cut into cubes
1 medium zucchini, halved and sliced into 1 cm-thick pieces
cherry tomatoes

For the marinade:
4 tbsp oyster sauce
3 tbsp honey
2 tbsp soy sauce
2 tbsp sesame oil
2 tbsp rice wine
6 garlic cloves, chopped

Khmer Beef Lok Lak

Serves 4

~ 2 tbsp vegetable oil ~ 4 garlic cloves, chopped ~ 400g beef tenderloin, cubed ~ 4 tbsp oyster sauce ~ 4 tbsp Chinese wine or dry sherry ~ 1½ cups beef stock, mixed with 1 tbsp corn flour ~ 1 tsp sugar ~ salt and pepper to taste ~

For the garnish:
~ bunch of lettuce leaves ~ 1 red onion, thinly sliced ~ 4 tomatoes, sliced ~

For the dipping sauce:
~ juice of 1 large lime ~ salt to taste and lots of cracked black pepper ~

Heat oil in a wok. Add garlic and fry until golden. Add beef and fry for 2-3 minutes. Add wine and beef stock mixture and cook for 2 more minutes. Prepare a large serving plate with lettuce, onions and tomatoes to one side and serve the lok lak next to it, with the dipping sauce on the side.

Try with: Fried rice and an ice-cold beer -- that's the way Khmers like it.

See page 16

Khmer Vegetable Fried Rice

~ 4 tbsp vegetable oil ~ 3 garlic cloves, chopped ~ 1 medium carrot, peeled and finely diced ~ 1 small bunch Chinese or French green beans, sliced ~ 2 stalks of Chinese broccoli (*kai lan*), peeled and sliced ~ 2 tbsp tomato sauce ~ 2 tbsp chilli sauce ~ 2 tbsp soy sauce ~ 2 tbsp oyster sauce ~ 6 cups of steamed jasmine rice ~ spring onions and fresh coriander, chopped ~

Heat oil in wok. Add garlic and fry until golden. Add all the vegetables and fry for 2 more minutes. Stir in tomato, chilli, soy and oyster sauces. Add steamed rice and fry for 2 more minutes. Divide between 4 plates and garnish with spring onions and coriander.

Relishes and Dressings

All recipes make 4-6 servings

Apple and Cranberry Relish

2 cups fresh or frozen
cranberries, *not* canned
2 Granny Smith apples,
unpeeled, cored and diced
½ lemon, unpeeled, diced and
seeded
1 orange, unpeeled, diced and
seeded
juice of 1 lemon
2 tbsp brown sugar
1 tsp English mustard

Place all the ingredients into a
food processor and pulse until it
resembles a relish. Chill.

Try with: Roast turkey or ham. In
the restaurant we serve it on our
chicken burger.

Orange and Sesame Dressing

1 cup fresh orange juice
$1/3$ cup sesame oil
$1/4$ cup rice vinegar
3 tbsp soy sauce
2 tbsp sugar syrup
1 tsp ginger, grated
1 small chilli, seeded and
chopped

Place all the ingredients into a
glass jar with a lid and shake well.

Try with: Mixed greens, such
as rocket, radicchio and chicory,
topped with orange segments
and sesame seeds as a starter.
Or drizzle over grilled chicken for
a light lunch.

Mango and Coriander Salsa

2 medium ripe mangoes, peeled
and diced
2 medium tomatoes, peeled,
seeded and diced
½ green pepper, diced
4 Asian shallots, peeled and
diced
1 small bunch coriander,
chopped
1 Tabasco splash
juice of 1 lime
½ tsp sugar, if needed
salt and pepper to taste

Gently mix all ingredients together
and refrigerate for 1 hour.

Try with: Any kind of white meat or
fish, or serve with taco chips. At the
restaurant, we serve it on a smoked
chicken breast sandwich, and
sometimes with grilled pork chops.

Apple Cider Vinaigrette with **Pumpkin Seed Oil**

½ cup apple cider vinegar
½ cup pumpkin seed oil
(available in specialty stores)
1 tsp sugar
salt and pepper to taste

Place all ingredients into a glass jar with a lid and shake well.

Try with: A tomato and red onion salad, mixed salad, or an Austrian sausage salad.

Tip: Pumpkin seed oil can only be used raw, not for cooking. It is expensive but a little goes a long way.

Papaya and **Mint Relish**

1 medium ripe papaya, about 500g, peeled and diced
3 medium Asian shallots, peeled and diced
1½ cups mint, chopped
juice of 1 large lime
1 Tabasco splash
salt and pepper to taste

Gently mix all ingredients together and refrigerate for 1 hour.

Try with: Grilled fish or chicken, or serve with taro or sweet potato chips along with drinks.

Roasted Garlic and Red Wine Vinaigrette

1 head garlic cloves
1 tsp olive oil
½ cup extra virgin olive oil
½ cup red wine vinegar
½ cup herbs, such as thyme, basil and marjoram, chopped
1 tsp sugar
salt and pepper to taste

Cut the top off the garlic head and place on a baking tray. Drizzle with olive oil and bake on medium heat for about 25 minutes. Set aside to cool. Pop the garlic cloves out of their skins and mash.

Place the mash and remaining ingredients into a glass jar with a lid and shake well.

Try with: All kinds of green vegetables, or as an accompaniment to roast lamb or beef.

des

"A lot of people order desserts to
share. Normally they're skinny women."

Kim Heuorn, 19, waiter

Sticky Rice with Yellow Bean on Sweet Mango Sauce

For the yellow bean paste:
$^2/_3$ cup yellow beans, soaked for 1 hour in
cold water
1 tbsp sugar
pinch of salt

For the rice:
2 cups sticky rice flour
$^2/_3$ cup hot water

For the mango sauce:
2 large mangoes
1 tbsp sugar syrup
1 tsp fresh lime juice

For the topping:
2 tbsp fresh shredded coconut
1 tsp each of black and white sesame seeds
1 tbsp castor sugar

Add enough water to just cover the yellow beans and bring to boil with the sugar and salt.

Boil until the liquid has evaporated, which should take about 1 hour. Set aside to cool. Shape into 2cm rugby-ball shapes.

Spoon the hot water slowly into the rice flour and knead until smooth, then shape into small balls.

Flatten the balls with the heel of your hand and place a bean paste ball in the centre of each.
Roll between your palms to resemble a sausage roll. Boil for about 20 minutes and set aside to cool.

For the sauce, blend the mangoes, syrup and lime juice in a food processor.

Pour the sauce onto a large plate.

Place the rolls on top, and sprinkle with the topping ingredients. **Makes about 20 pieces.**

butter and flour for greasing
180g unsalted butter,
softened to room
temperature
180g white sugar
6 eggs
zest of 4 large limes
240g fresh coconut
180g self-raising flour, sifted
2 tsp baking powder

For the syrup:
pulp of 8 passionfruit
6 tbsp sugar syrup

Preheat the oven to 200°C or gas 6. Grease and flour a 22cm round cake tin.

Cream butter and sugar until light and fluffy, then slowly add eggs, one at a time, beating well after each. Stir in lime zest and coconut, and mix well. Fold in the flour and baking powder and mix until well combined.

Spoon mixture into the cake tin and bake for 40-45 minutes.

Allow cake to cool. Combine syrup ingredients and pour over cake to serve. **Serves 8-10.**

Try with: Vanilla ice cream.

Coconut Lime Cake with Passionfruit Syrup

Friends' Blueberry Cake

"When I look at the menu, all I can see is that blueberry cake! "

Kut Pisey, 22, waiter

butter for greasing
390g can sweetened condensed milk
1 cup sugar
2 eggs
pinch salt
2 tbsp vegetable oil
3 cups plain flour
1 tsp baking powder
1½ cups fresh or frozen blueberries, not canned
icing sugar

For the syrup:
2 tsp sugar
3 tsp fresh lime juice
1 tsp cinnamon powder

↗375-(400) (for 35 to 40 min)

Preheat oven to 200ºC or gas 6. Grease a 22cm round cake tin with butter. Mix milk, sugar, eggs, salt and oil until creamy. Mix flour and baking powder and gently fold into milk mixture. Pour half of the mixture into the cake tin and top with blueberries. Pour the remainder of the cake mixture on top. Mix syrup ingredients and drizzle over the cake. Bake for 45 minutes. Cool and sprinkle with icing sugar.

Try with: Vanilla ice cream.

Serves 8-10

Friends' Chocolate and Almond Cake

butter and flour for greasing
250g unsalted butter
340g high-quality dark chocolate
100g almond flour
100g plain flour
100g sugar
6 eggs, separated
fresh mint, for garnish

For the sauce:
300g fresh raspberries
1 shot raspberry liqueur
.3 tbsp lemon juice
6 tbsp sugar syrup

Preheat oven to 200ºC or gas 6. Blend the sauce ingredients in a food processor until smooth and place in the fridge.

Grease and flour a 22cm round cake tin. Melt the butter and chocolate over a steam bath and set aside.

In another bowl, mix together the flours, sugar and egg yolks. Slowly add the chocolate mixture into the egg yolk mixture. Beat the egg whites until stiff and slowly fold into the main mixture. Spoon into tin and bake for 40 minutes. Do not overbake! It's fine if the cake is still a little sticky in the centre.

Allow the cake to cool. Serve with the raspberry sauce, garnished with mint.

Try with: Vanilla ice cream and a good espresso.

Serves 10-12

friends

Banana Fritters with Lime Syrup

1 cup self-raising flour
1 tsp baking powder
1 tbsp sugar
1 pinch salt
1 large egg, beaten
¾ cup milk
1 tbsp butter, melted
12 small bananas, or 4 bananas, cut in half
oil for deep frying
icing sugar

For the syrup:
4 cups sugar syrup
juice of 1 medium lime
zest of 1 lime

Serves 4

For the batter, mix all the dry ingredients together. In a separate bowl, combine the egg, milk and melted butter and slowly stir the dry ingredients in.

Dip the bananas into the batter and deep fry at 375ºC until golden, which should take about 2 minutes. Drain on paper towels.

For the syrup, mix the sugar syrup, juice and zest together. Drizzle over the bananas, dust with icing sugar and serve immediately.

Try with: Vanilla ice cream. You can use apples or pineapple instead of banana if you prefer, but banana is the MOST delicious!

f r i e n d s

Apple, Almond and **Bread Pudding**

Serves 8-10

~ butter for greasing ~ 6 eggs ~
1 cup fresh milk or cream ~ 1 tsp
cinnamon ~ 1 tsp nutmeg ~ 1 tsp
allspice ~ 1 cup brown sugar ~ 1
tsp vanilla essence ~ ½ tsp almond essence ~ 250g white bread,
cubed ~ 1 cup raisins ~ 4 Granny
Smith apples, peeled and diced ~

Preheat oven to 200ºC or gas 6. Grease
a 22cm round cake tin. In a bowl, whisk
together eggs, milk, spices, sugar and
vanilla and almond essences. In another
bowl, spread bread, raisins and apples,
and pour the milk mixture over them. Let
soak for 20 minutes. Spoon into the cake
tin and bake for 40-45 minutes.

Try with: Vanilla sauce.

"When I was learning to make the chocolate mousse, I put the wrong whipping cream into the mixture and ruined 26 servings. I felt very sorry for my teacher, who luckily wasn't angry. So my tip for making this mousse is: use the right cream."

Sok Rany, 23, graduate

Chocolate and Amaretto Mousse

**~ 375g high-quality dark chocolate ~ 8 eggs, separated ~ ½ cup sugar ~
60 ml amaretto or frangelico ~ 1 cup whipping cream ~**

Melt chocolate in a bowl over a steam bath and set aside. In another bowl, beat egg yolks with the sugar until creamy. Slowly add mixture and amaretto to melted chocolate and gently combine.

Whip cream and gently fold into chocolate mixture.

Beat egg whites until stiff and stir into main mixture. Refrigerate for at least 4 hours or overnight.

Try with: The raspberry sauce on page 98. This mousse is to die for!

Serves 8-10

Shakes & Freezes

Margaritas & Daiquiris

Passionfruit and Vanilla Shake

pulp of 2 passionfruit

4 scoops vanilla ice cream

2 tbsp condensed milk

juice of 1 lime

juice of 1 orange

3 tbsp sugar syrup

$^1/_3$ cup fresh milk or yoghurt

3 cups crushed ice

Blend all ingredients for 1-2 minutes.
Serve immediately.

Serves 2

Strawberry and Soursop Shake

½ cup soursop, peeled, seeded and diced

6 fresh or frozen strawberries

2 tbsp condensed milk

2 tbsp sugar syrup

juice of 1 lime

juice of 1 orange

1 tbsp strawberry syrup

3 cups crushed ice

Blend all ingredients except ice for 1 minute.
Add ice and blend until slushy.
Serve immediately.

Serves 2

*"I always recommend that customers try soursop... It's so delicious!
It's nicely bitter, has a great aroma and is also really good for your skin."*

Chuon Veary, 18, waiter

friends

Coconut Lime Shake

$^1/_3$ **cup coconut juice or milk**

juice of 1 lime

juice of 1 orange

2 tbsp condensed milk

2 tbsp sugar syrup

3 cups crushed ice

fresh mint, for garnish

Blend all ingredients for 1-2 minutes. Serve immediately, garnished with fresh mint.

Serves 2

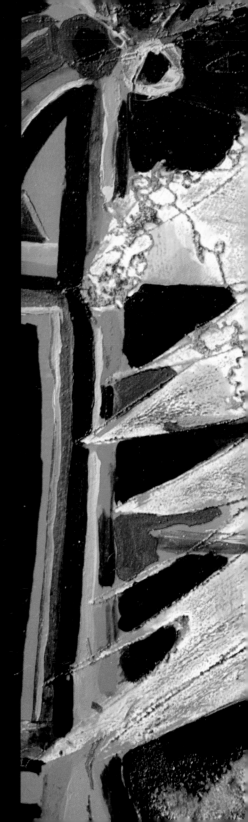

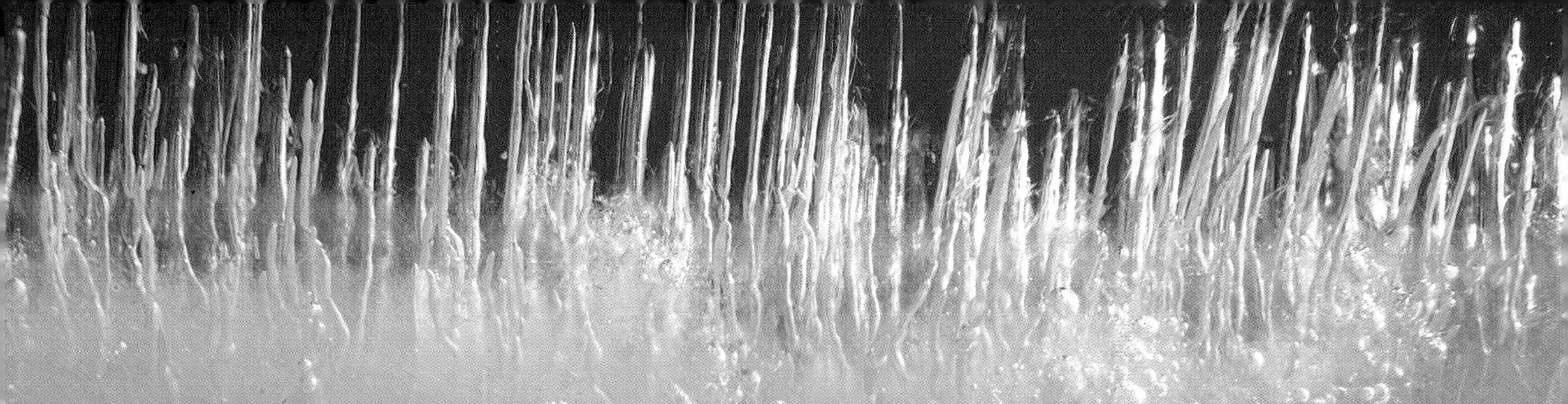

Watermelon and Passion-fruit Freeze

2 large chunks of watermelon, peeled and seeded
pulp of 2 passionfruit
juice of ½ lime
juice of 1 orange
2 tbsp sugar syrup
3 cups crushed ice

Green Apple and Lime Freeze

1 large Granny Smith apple, seeded and cut into quarters
juice of 1 orange
juice of 1 lime
2 tbsp sugar syrup
3 cups crushed ice

Citrus and Mint Freeze

juice of 2 limes
juice of 2 oranges
juice of 1 lemon
1 cup fresh mint, roughly chopped
4 tbsp sugar syrup
3 cups crushed ice

Blend all ingredients except ice for 1 minute. Add ice and blend until slushy. Serve immediately.

Serves 2

Yu Kim Daron

Sun Senon   Chea Savon

Chom Kunthea

Some graduates

Mean Piset

Chan Veasna

Sok Rany

I was about to finish my training course and went to see the placement officer. "So, how can I help you?" he started. I told him that I would like to discuss my business plan with him. He said that I was right to come and see him because since I had only finished level 2 of cooking class, I had three options: to leave and get a job, to leave and start up a small business running a food stall, or to continue with level 3 cookery. After our discussion, I decided to continue my studies because in the long run it would help me to get a better job. So at that point, I went to work in Friends The Restaurant. It was a good day to start my training at that level because there was a big party in the restaurant. Everybody was busy running around serving the customers -- it was a tiring day but interesting too. I got back to the Friends Residential Centre quite late and immediately fell asleep. At the end of the month, I received some money for my in-service training plus my cut of the tips! I like my training very much and hope that one day I will be able to have a job like this too.

Both my parents died of HIV/AIDS, leaving me alone. I didn't want to stay with any of my relatives -- they were either poor or mean. Besides, I felt old enough to look after myself. So I started to work on the streets, but it was hard and I soon realised that living and working like that had no future. I met with Friends social workers and was encouraged to visit the centre and learn a vocational skill. I chose cookery training because I want to become a chef. They also promised to prepare a 'family memory book' for me and I gave them some photos of my parents. When I saw the book, I was very happy.

My life has become much better since I moved from living on the streets to stay at Friends. I have become a student and a son within the big family at the Residential Centre. My two younger sisters, who used to beg and scavenge on the streets of Phnom Penh, also came. When we were living on the streets, we met Friends social workers and they asked us to visit the centre. We were shown all the Friends services and encouraged to come back. We agreed and I was happy to stay there because it is safe and friendly. Now, my sisters and I can read and write and I know that we will be able to continue our education.

Yesterday was a good day! One of my former classmates, who graduated from Friends 3 months ago, came back to visit the sewing class. She was there to reimburse the loan given to her by Friends. During the lunch break we went to the market and she bought some things for her business, then we had ice cream and returned to class. She spent half an hour explaining how successful her business had become, which was of real encouragement to the rest of us. I now want to work even harder because I want to have the same success.

I come from a rural area of Prey Veng province. My family are very poor. My parents are farmers and like most girls in the area, I quit school when I was 12 to start helping them in the fields. Work was very hard. I worked all day under a hot sun or in heavy rain. But I wanted something better and heard that in Phnom Penh girls could get jobs in garment factories, so along with three other girls from the village, I headed to the city to look for work. We rented a small room in the squatter district but after only a few days, realised that Phnom Penh wasn't as safe as we had first thought. It was also difficult to get a job because the factory managers only wanted people with sewing skills, and none of us had them. Two of the girls decided to go back to the provinces and I was about to do the same when I met a Friends social worker on the streets who talked to me about a future plan through Friends. I decided to try and get sewing skills and was allowed to stay in the Residential Centre throughout my short-term training programme. I now have a job in a factory and was recently able to visit my parents. They were very happy!

Pineapple and Chilli Margarita

Serves 1

30 ml Cointreau
45 ml tequila
1 slice pineapple
1 Tabasco splash
30ml fresh lime juice
30ml sugar syrup
1 cup crushed ice
salt and lime wedge
1 small red chilli, for garnish

Blend Cointreau, tequila, pineapple, Tabasco, lime juice and sugar syrup. Add crushed ice and blend until slushy. Pour into margarita glass frosted with lime and salt and garnish with chilli.

"A margarita is best enjoyed on its own. I recommend one before a meal, or three, maximum, if you're not eating."

Keo Phearun, 21, graduate

friends

Mandarin and Mango Daiquiri

Mandarin and Mango Daiquiri. 60ml good quality rum, ½ mango, peeled or cut into cubes, or equivalent in frozen puree, 30ml mandarin juice, 30ml lime juice, 30ml sugar syrup, 1 cup crushed ice. Blend rum, mango, mandarin juice, lime juice, and sugar syrup. Add crushed ice and blend for a further 20 seconds. Pour into glass nd garnish with a fresh sprig of mint and a mandarin slice.

Serves 1

Raspberry and Lime Daiquiri

60 ml good-quality rum
30 ml fresh lime juice
30 ml sugar syrup
$^1/_3$ cup frozen raspberries
1 tsp raspberry syrup, optional
1 cup crushed ice

Blend rum, lime juice, syrups and raspberries. Add crushed ice and blend until slushy. Pour into a chilled cocktail glass and serve immediately.

Serves 1

~ Acknowledgments ~

The contributors and Mith Samlanh/Friends would like to thank the following people for their involvement in the making of this cookbook:

Rogier van Anholt, Sok Barang, Sharee Bauld, Kun Boren, Duk Chandany, Chhung Chhandara, Sok Chhong, Darryl Collins, Lang Dana, Keo Dara, Nget Dara, Yu Kim Daron, Elizabeth Holland, Kheng Khemara, Sot Kimyuri, Roath Kosal, Sok Krimheaun, Chom Kunthea, Pierre-Louis Leroy, Sarah Lowing, Ou Makdarin, David Marshall, Sian Martin, Stuart McDonald, Sok Nina, Kee Chong Peoung, Srun Pheakdey, Phy Pichleakena, Marlou Pijnappel, Mean Piset, Khatt Pisey, Sok Rany, Doung Rathanak, Tree Rith, Nicolas Rambaud, Reoun Ry, Sok Sameourn, Sey Samnang, Sal San, Phann Sarah, Yin Sarat, Phatt Saren, Phann Sari, Chea Savon, So Savuth, Sun Senon, Sao Sokunthy, Phatt Sony, Cheng Sophal, Beng Sophany, Meen Sopheap, Kroach Sophig, Kim Sophorn, Pho Sophorn, Earng Sotivi, Som Sovannita, Toun Soviet, Ni Teoun, Roath Theary, Srang Theavy, Kit Va, That Va, Ngin Vanna, Chourn Vary, Chan Veasna, Kak Vichay, Elfriede Wolfsberger, and finally the art teacher, Chorn Channavath and all his students in Club Friends for providing the wonderful paintings throughout this book.

Friends The Restaurant is sponsored by the following donors and would like to thank them for their continued support:

European Commission

Kosal ~ Boren ~ Dana ~ Sophorn ~ Sovieth ~ Rith ~ Sophom ~ Pisey ~ Dara ~ Pheakday ~ Theavy

Socheat ~ San ~ Darlin ~ Sara ~ Sokly ~ Theary ~ Saren ~ Samnang ~ Veary ~ Khemara ~ Sony ~ Gustav

Sok Heng ~ Sopheap ~ Rathanak ~ Rathanak ~ Sarry ~ Savuth ~ Bunsun ~ Nina ~ Sotheavy ~ Sokunthy ~ Vanna ~ Chhong

Theoun ~ Dara ~ Phanny ~ Dani ~ Kim Heoun ~ Ry ~ Sarat ~ Sam Eorn ~ Va ~ Anita ~ Darin

stir-fried clams with tamarind and spicy basil 58
Friends' famous Khmer chicken curry 71

papaya~
Khmer pork and papaya salad sandwich 76
v papaya and mint relish 89

paprika~
mixed greens with prawns in cumin and coriander dressing 64

parsley~
mixed greens with prawns in cumin and coriander dressing 64

passionfruit~
v coconut lime cake with passionfruit syrup 94
v passionfruit and vanilla shake 108
v watermelon and passionfruit freeze 113

pasta~
v grilled vegetable and pasta salad with goat cheese 26

peanuts~
Khmer fish soup with tamarind 26
marinated fish salad with lime and coriander 55

pepper~
v grilled vegetable and pasta salad with goat cheese 26
v Asian-style mango coleslaw with sesame and lime 30
fish and potato cakes with roasted red pepper sauce 48 marinated fish salad with lime and coriander 55
v mango and coriander salsa 88

pineapple~
v pineapple and chilli margarita 119

pomelo~
pomelo salad with grilled chicken and fresh mint 72

pork~
Khmer pork and papaya salad sandwich 76
honey garlic meatballs 82

potato~
v sweet potato fries with curry mayonnaise 36
fish and potato cakes with roasted red pepper sauce 48

Friends' famous Khmer chicken curry 71

prawn~
crispy prawn wontons with sweet chilli sauce 46
Khmer seafood soup with lime 56
mixed greens with prawns in cumin and coriander dressing 64

pumpkin~
v curried pumpkin soup with coriander 25

R

raisin~
v apple, almond and bread pudding 103

raspberry~
v Friends' chocolate and almond cake 98
v raspberry and lime daiquiri 121
  liqueur~
v Friends' chocolate and almond cake 98

relishes~
mango and coriander salsa 88
apple and cranberry 88
papaya and mint 89

rice~
  jasmine~
Khmer vegetable fried rice 14, 86
  paper~
v mushroom and leek spring rolls with lemon mayonnaise 34

rum~
v mandarin and mango daiquiri 119
v raspberry and lime daiquiri 121

S

salads~
v grilled vegetable and pasta salad with goat cheese 26
v grilled eggplant salad with toasted coconut 33
mixed greens with prawns in cumin and coriander dressing 64
marinated fish salad with lime and coriander 55
pomelo salad with grilled chicken and fresh mint 72

scallops~
Khmer seafood soup with lime 56
sesame seeds~
v Asian-style mango coleslaw with sesame and lime 30

v sticky rice with yellow bean on sweet mango sauce 93

sesame oil~
v Asian-style mango coleslaw with sesame and lime 30
Asian-style chicken and veggie kebabs 85
v orange and sesame dressing 88

shakes~
v passionfruit and vanilla 108
v strawberry and soursop 109
v coconut lime 110

shrimp paste~
Khmer fish soup with tamarind 42
Friends' famous Khmer chicken curry 71

soup~
v curried pumpkin soup with coriander 25
Khmer fish soup with tamarind 42
Cambodian seafood soup with lime 56

soursop~
v strawberry and soursop shake 109

soy sauce~
honey garlic meatballs 82
Asian-style chicken and veggie kebabs 85
v Khmer vegetable fried rice 14, 86
v orange and sesame dressing 88

star anise powder~
Friends' famous Khmer chicken curry 71

sticky rice flour~
v sticky rice with yellow bean on sweet mango sauce 93

stock~
v curried pumpkin soup with coriander (chicken or vegetable) 25
Khmer fish soup with tamarind (seafood or vegetable) 42
Khmer seafood soup with lime (chicken or seafood) 56
stir-fried clams with tamarind and spicy basil (clam or chicken) 58
mixed greens with prawns in cumin and coriander dressing (prawn) 64
Friends' famous Khmer chicken curry 71
chicken, mango and cashew stir-fry (chicken) 81
Khmer beef lok lak (beef) 14, 86

strawberry~
v strawberry and soursop shake 109

sweet potato~
v sweet potato fries with curry mayonnaise 36

T

Tabasco~
fish and potato cakes with roasted red pepper sauce 48
v mango and coriander salsa 88
v papaya and mint relish 89
v pineapple and chilli margarita 118

tahini~
v sun-dried tomato hummus on crispy wonton wrappers 21

tamarind~
Khmer fish soup with tamarind 42
Khmer seafood soup with lime 56
stir-fried clams with tamarind and spicy basil 58

tequila~
v pineapple and chilli margarita 118

tomato~
v Friends' famous smoky eggplant dip 23
v grilled vegetable and pasta salad with goat's cheese 26
v stir-fried tomato wedges with mint 28
grilled fish with salsa verde 52
lemon and garlic squid 63
Friends' grilled steak sandwich 77
Asian-style chicken and veggie kebabs 85
Khmer beef lok lak 14, 86
v mango and coriander salsa 88
  paste~
honey garlic meatballs 82
  sauce~
honey garlic meatballs 82
v Khmer vegetable fried rice 14, 86
  sun-dried~
v sun-dried tomato hummus on crispy wonton wrappers 21

turmeric~
v curried pumpkin soup with coriander 25
Khmer fish soup with tamarind 42
Friends' famous Khmer chicken curry 71

V

vanilla essence~
v apple, almond and bread pudding 103

vinegar~
  apple cider~
v apple cider vinaigrette with pumpkin seed oil 89
  red wine~
v grilled vegetable and pasta salad with goat cheese 26
fish and potato cakes with roasted red pepper sauce 48
mixed greens with prawns in cumin and coriander dressing 64
v roasted garlic and red wine vinaigrette 89
  rice~
v grilled eggplant salad with toasted coconut 33
pomelo salad with grilled chicken and fresh mint 72
v orange and sesame dressing 88
  sherry~
grilled fish with salsa verde 52

W

watermelon~
v watermelon and passionfruit freeze 113

wine~
  Chinese~
stir-fried clams with tamarind and spicy basil 58
chicken, mango and cashew nut stir-fry 81
Khmer beef lok lak 14, 86
  rice~
Asian-style chicken and veggie kebabs 85

wonton wrappers~
v sun-dried tomato hummus on crispy wonton wrappers 21
crispy prawn wontons with sweet chilli sauce 46

Worcestershire sauce~
v mushroom and leek spring rolls with lemon mayonnaise 34
lemon and garlic squid 63
honey garlic meatballs 82

Y

yoghurt~
v passionfruit and vanilla shake 108

Z

zucchini~
v grilled vegetable and pasta salad with goat cheese 26
Asian-style chicken and veggie kebabs 85